BETTER DAYS
A Mental Health Recovery Workbook

Craig Lewis, CPS

Better Days Recovery Press

Better Days: A Mental Health Recovery Workbook, Third Edition
© 2014 by Craig Lewis. All Rights Reserved
The forms in this book may be copied for personal use and as handouts for support group members. If any of the materials in this book are to be copied or used in any other document or in any other way—either in print, audio, or electronically—permission must be obtained in advance from Craig Lewis. You can reach him at: betterdaysrecovery@gmail.com
Copying and distributing portions of this book without citing the source is a violation of copyright. Copying and distributing this book in part or in its entirety is a violation of copyright, with the exceptions listed above. Sale of materials from this work without permission is not permitted.
ISBN: 978-1-312-22532-9
Published by Better Days Recovery Press
Edited by Carrie Keeler
Production edited by Jonathan Rowland
Photo courtesy of Max Braverman
Technical Assistance by Colin Hennigar
Cover Design by Jennifer McMahon, JenniferChristineMcMahon@gmail.com
Printed in the United States of America

This workbook is dedicated to Laurie Rose, Alison Kempson Aparicio, Lisha Weeks, Domenic Stagno, and Scott Forman. Without each and every one of you, I would not have learned what it means to have a Better Day. You have changed my life forever, and now I get to help other people make their lives better. Being alive and well is a dream come true, and this workbook is the guide with which I live every Better Day. For all the people who are fighting for their recovery, this workbook is also dedicated to you. I believe in all of you.

Table of Contents

Introduction 1
Foreword 3
Sometimes We Struggle 5
Accountability 7
Am I OK? 9
Being Self-Aware 11
Biting Your Tongue 13
Coping Skills 15
Creating Change 17
Dealing with Injustice 19
Feeling Good 21
Fun and Enjoyment 23
Getting Our Needs Met 25
Our Lives Have Value 27
Passing Moments 29
Recovery is Wonderful 31
Recovery Planning 33
Staying Strong 35
Ups and Downs 37
We Can't Control Everything 39
Being in the Moment 41
Dealing with the Impossible 43
Having Patience 45
The Importance of Companionship 47
Living the Life You Want to Live 49
Meaningful Activities 51
Resiliency 53
The Little Things 55
Time Management 57
Working through Pain 59
The Value in Our Struggle 61
The Phoenix Will Always Rise 63
Doing Something Nice for Yourself 65
Expectations 67
Gratitude List 69

Frustration 71
Choosing Better Ways to React..73
Getting Upset..75

Introduction

In this Better Days recovery workbook, we talk about various situations and rough spots in our lives and the ways we can stay on board to get to the better life that we want. Sometimes, when a difficult situation comes up, our daily lives can be disrupted. This workbook can help us achieve the better life we want by exploring some ways that we can make the best of our days, even when things that are happening are not so great. By going through this process, we can be better prepared for the times when things are difficult so that we can get closer to living the life we want, step by step.

My life has been improving step by step. I didn't get to my better life overnight. It took time and hard work. It took dedication and perseverance. It took making mistakes and learning from those mistakes. It took celebrating my successes, even if they were minor, and applauding them.

To choose: to decide to do something.

Every day we have to choose how we want to live. We can choose to work hard and we can choose to try our best. Ultimately, it is up to each and every one of us to decide how our day is going to be. We wake up in the morning, we shower and get dressed, we eat something and we go out to start our day. We can look inward for a moment to see what gets us to do these things. Is it a choice we are making? Or is there something stronger taking us and moving us forward on our path? Are the choices that we are making part of a simple routine that we embark upon on a daily basis and, if so, are they rooted deep within us? Are we, as human beings, built in such a way that it is our natural, mental and physical desire to make healthy choices? If it is, does this mean that, when we work on improving ourselves even in very small ways, this is what our body and mind naturally wants for us, even if we have some sort of mental health condition that makes things more complicated? Does this mean that even with having a mental health condition that our desires to be successful and happy and to live a fulfilled life can be realized? I think we are all living proof of this so let's make today and everyday a Better Day.

I would like to share with you the history of Better Days. When I first began my recovery journey I attended a school called the Consumer Provider Program in Somerville, Massachusetts. This was a college accredited two semester program that included the Certified Peer Specialist training. I received a fantastic education in how to provide quality support for people like me, people that live with mental health struggles, addiction, and trauma. One requirement of this educational process was that I needed to complete a 300 hour internship. Thankfully, I was able to do my internship at the Michael J. Gill Rehabilitation Center in Jamaica Plain, MA. As part of my time at Gill I needed to "leave something behind," which meant to create something that would remain at the program once I had completed my 300 hours. I decided to try to develop a peer support group and proposed the concept of Better Days. I made a flyer to get the word out and about twenty people attended. It was a smashing success. I developed new curricula each week and the people who attended reported that they were benefiting from the group. After I completed my internship, I worked at a peer led program for a year and gave the group there and then volunteered for two years giving the group at the Boston Resource Center. People continued to say that they were benefiting from the curriculum, which was wonderful for both them and me. Two years ago I decided to stop my volunteering as I became too busy and the curriculum sat in a draw unused. I then had the thought to try and put all my work into book form and did so with the help of others. Since publishing this workbook, hundreds of people from all over the world have been ordering copies for personal use and to use in support groups and the response I have received has been overwhelmingly positive. For me this experience is extremely fulfilling as I get to bask in the reality that something I created with the purest of intentions, which was to help others while processing my own struggles, is now benefiting hundreds of people worldwide as they travel on their recovery journeys. This Better Days workbook has changed my life forever and I hope you will embrace it and allow it to help you do the same.

–Craig Lewis

Foreword

In the recovery process, nothing can replace the value of peer-to-peer support.

Not even therapy from the most skilled, credentialed professional could ever replace the power of that peer-topeer connection. There is just something incredibly powerful from the level of guidance you can receive from a person who identifies as a survivor and is willing to guide you down the paths that on which he has journeyed. Craig Lewis provides that survivor's guidance in his brilliantly constructed workbook, Better Days: A Mental Health Recovery Workbook. Craig's candidness and unique perspective makes this book an incredibly valuable asset to your recovery toolbox.

I do not make this recommendation lightly. As an individual in recovery from both addiction and depression related to traumatic stress, I've worked through my share of recovery workbooks. I am also a professional working, teaching, and writing in the field, and I've read, reviewed, and even written my share of books and manuals. Craig gives us something special in Better

Days. First, I find that the workbook serves as a wonderful guide if you want to keep a journal but don't really know where to start. Perhaps your previous attempts at journaling have not proven very therapeutic because you find yourself just beating yourself up with your words. While many helpers and counselors will advise their clients to "Keep a journal," Craig gives you the practical guidance on how to write in a way that is both releasing and proactive.

Developing a toolbox of active, dynamic coping skills is absolutely important to people in recovery from both addiction and mental health struggles. Too often, the problems with which we struggle are made worse by going too deeply into our thoughts and obsessing over them instead of making and working a clear plan of action for how to deal with them. Craig helps you do this in a very gentle way by first validating and normalizing the variety of struggles that come with recovery, and then practically guiding you to make and work a plan.

The workbook is set-up so that you can work through it at your own pace. You can also skim through it and work the individual exercises/themes in a way that suits what you are addressing in your recovery at any given moment. Each of the exercises, although written in human, practical terms, are informed by some of our most innovative knowledge from the field on what can work to heal traumas (wounds), mental health struggles, and addiction. In my teachings, I contend that safety and flexibility are the two traits of what makes healing strategies trauma-informed. Craig really honors a commitment to both values in his work.

I've only had the pleasure of recently making Craig's acquaintance, yet I am already looking forward to working with and collaborating more with him over the years. I believe that he and his work represent a much-needed voice of experience, strength, hope, reality, and recovery that we need in our treatment fields and in the healing arts in general. His ability to "keep it real" is the major reason I value his voice so highly. Recovery is a struggle, and Craig communicates this in a very effective way. Yet recovery is also a treasured new life that Craig Lewis clearly appreciates, and has a gift for helping people claim and accept this treasure. My clients will benefit from the use of this workbook, and I plan on enthusiastically recommending it to trainees for years to come.

Jamie Marich, Ph.D., LPCC-S, LICDC-CS

Author of Trauma Made Simple:

Competencies in Assessment, Treatment, and Working with Survivors; Trauma and the Twelve Steps; Creative Mindfulness; and EMDR Made Simple.

Creator of the Dancing Mindfulness

Practice

www.jamiemarich.com

www.mindfulohio.com

www.dancingmindfulness.com

Sometimes We Struggle

There are days when I feel so bad that I become unable to see things for how they really are. Often my thoughts are twisting and turning throughout a maze of total and brutal negativity. I find myself gasping for air and grasping for a hand to hold onto, yet sometimes it seems that I am very alone.

I ask myself——is this struggle for wellness and recovery worthy of all my efforts? Why am I dedicating all my hard work and time and effort toward my recovery? What is this recovery that I am fighting so hard for?

It is important for us to think of the big picture. When we work hard to improve our quality of life and strengthen our coping skills, we will experience beneficial results. When we struggle, experience difficulties and question our recovery, we can and will take back our lives and celebrate our progress and accept that sometimes, we will struggle.

Our struggle has meaning and our recovery is here to stay.

Notes:

Sometimes We Struggle Worksheet

1. Do you believe that there is meaning and value in your struggling and why?

2. In your daily life, how do you manage the ups and downs that you face without being thrown off course (give two examples)?

3. What are three reasons that you are fighting for your recovery?

Accountability

I have made countless mistakes over the course of my life. I have damaged others and I have damaged myself.

It is said that time heals all wounds. What does this mean? Is this true?

I think that taking responsibility for our actions can be an empowering process. Each of us possesses the ability to liberate ourselves from the chains of our past. The decisions that we make today and tomorrow are our gateway toward a Better Day and a better life.

Notes:

Accountability Worksheet

1. List three ways that your life has been affected by decisions that you have made.

2. Name one mistake that you have made in your life and what you learned because of it.

3. List three things that you want to improve in your life and what you can do to make them happen.

Am I OK?

I am OK.

I am doing just fine.

I am doing well.

Everything is under control.

Everything will be OK.

Everything is going to work out.

I can make improvements.

I can make adjustments.

I can get all my needs met.

I make all my choices.

I make all my decisions.

What happens to me is up to me.

I will survive.

I will thrive.

Victory will be mine.

Notes:

Am I OK? Worksheet

1. List three things that you like about yourself.

2. What does it mean to be gentle to yourself?

3. How does personal responsibility impact one's recovery?

Being Self-Aware

One of the most important components of mental health recovery is being self-aware.

What does it mean to be self-aware?

Are you aware of how you speak to people?

Are you aware of how others perceive you when you are communicating with them?

Are you aware of your body language and the message your body language sends to others?

Are you aware of your attitude?

Are you aware of how you are improving your life?

Are you aware of the things that you do that are causing you problems?

Can being self-aware help you to get to where you want to go in life?

Notes:

Being Self-Aware Worksheet

1. In what two ways are you self-aware?

2. What are two things that you know about yourself that you would like to change or improve?

3. How can being more self-aware make your life better?

Biting Your Tongue

Today I experienced the emotions of anger and hurt. My hurt feelings have been building up even while I have tried my best to process them. I could feel myself about to boil over like a pot on the stove.

I knew that I had to control myself. I knew that, as bad as I felt at that moment, that in time I would feel relief. I needed to protect myself and manage the intensity of what I was feeling and thinking.

I had to do this to protect myself so that I could deal with the issues responsibly once I felt more settled and calm. I had to bite my tongue in order to take care of myself and to protect my life. Only

I can do this for me, and only you can do it for you.

Notes:

Biting Your Tongue Worksheet

1. Name a situation where you had to bite your tongue and how your life benefited from you holding back your words.

2. What are three healthy ways that you can calm yourself down when you are angry?

3. When you are upset, hurt or angry, what can you say to those around you so that they can help you deal with your situation in more healthy ways?

Coping Skills

What are some of the problems that we must deal with in our daily lives? How do we cope with these problems?

For me, there are several things that I can do to help myself cope and feel better:

• I find that getting some exercise can really help me feel better. Why does exercise help one feel better? What different types of exercises can we do in our daily lives to feel better? How is exercising considered a coping skill?

• Sometimes I deal with the problems in my life by taking a nice hot shower or by listening to my favorite music.

• I can also ask someone to talk with me about how I am feeling or to talk about anything and get support from them. This is a great way to cope.

Notes:

Coping Skills Worksheet

1. What are three difficult things that you must cope with in your daily life?

2. What are three coping skills that you can use to manage the difficult situations in your life?

3. How do you define "Coping Skills"?

Creating Change

People say that change comes from within. This saying applies to most people, including people living with a mental health struggles.

What does it mean to change from within?

When I have something about myself or my life that I want to improve, I must work hard and implement changes in how I do things. I achieve this by focusing my thoughts on my goals and by taking healthy actions for change.

Mahatma Gandhi, the great Indian spiritual leader, said, "Be the change you want to see in the world." I say that first I must change myself into the person I want to be.

The ability to choose to change ourselves for the better is something that no one can take away from us. We can and we will live better lives, beginning with having a Better Day starting today.

Notes:

Creating Change Worksheet

1. What are the top three things that you want to change about yourself?

2. What good things have you gained from your struggle with your mental health?

3. What is the Number One thing that you can do today to improve your life for the better?

Dealing with Injustice

I live a life full of injustices, and I am a witness to injustices every single day.

What exactly is an injustice?

Having been institutionalized at age fourteen, I lived in hospitals, residential and group homes for many years. I was not taught how to take care of myself nor was I taught coping skills.

People who have trouble living in society are treated badly, even when it is not their choice or by their doing.

I would imagine that all the people using this workbook have suffered injustices in their lives.

A good thing is that we can better learn how to deal with the injustices in our lives and how we process our rage and pain. We can and will find better ways to live, and we can turn our pain into our strength.

We must be strong and work hard to rise above the injustices in our life.

Better Days are on the way and Better Days are here to stay.

Notes:

Dealing With Injustice Worksheet

1. Name an injustice that you have faced in your life and two ways that you can think you can better deal with how it makes you feel?

2. What are your top three best coping methods that you use when something very difficult has happened?

3. List one thing that you want to improve in your life and how you will achieve it.

Feeling Good

Wellness can arrive by surprise. The gap between struggling and satisfaction is thin. Recovery exists within all of us when we are struggling; it can keep us alert and focused on the future.

I had been struggling for several weeks. Recently, I could feel my mind shift toward my Better

Days. This caused me to smile more and be nicer to people. It got me to feel more calm, gentle and compassionate. It nurtured my thinking into a healthier process.

I sang in the shower.

I laughed and I smiled and I made jokes.

When I feel good it is great and when I don't feel so good I can try harder until I get to my Better

Day.

Recovery gives me wings and I feel beautiful.

Notes:

Feeling Good Worksheet

1. In what ways do you know that you are starting to feel well when you are?

2. Do you believe that recovery exists within you when you are struggling?

3. Give an example of something you do when you are feeling great.

Fun and Enjoyment

As a person living with a mental health struggle, I know that I am often so busy trying to get my needs met that I don't get to do much that is fun. It seems that the system focuses more on treatment and the management of people's lives. The result of this is that not very much attention is put toward doing fun and enjoyable things.

Some things that I like to do are going to the movies, going for a nice walk or sharing a nice meal with good friends.

Sometimes when things are really tough for me, I seem to forget how to have fun and do enjoyable things that please me.

I believe that we all deserve to live a good quality life and that we are all worthy of having fun and enjoyment in our lives. I believe that we all deserve to laugh and smile.

Notes:

Fun and Enjoyment Worksheet

1. List three things that you do in your life that are fun and enjoyable.

2. When did you last laugh and for what reason?

3. What are three ways in which your life can improve if you have more fun, more enjoyment, more smiling and more laughter in your life?

Getting Our Needs Met

Our lives can often be so difficult. We have to struggle to have a decent quality of life. My basic needs have so often not been met and, no matter how much I asked or begged for help, I felt ignored.

In the past, I have mostly yelled at or screamed at the people who were there to help me and while I yelled and screamed because no one would ever listen to me, it just made things worse. For me this is so frustrating because I am yelling and screaming to get my needs met because I want to be well.

However, if we can develop better ways to communicate what our needs are, then we will have our needs better met.

Recovery begins one Better Day at a time.

Notes:

Getting Our Needs Met Worksheet

1. What are three basic needs that you need or want to better address?

2. What are three helpful ways that we can communicate our needs to a doctor, a staff member, a family member, etc.?

3. What do you consider are effective ways to communicate?

Our Lives Have Value

As a person living with a mental health struggle, I have felt personally unfulfilled for most of my life.

While growing up, I watched a lot of the people I knew go to college, have relationships and become successful. At that same time, I was unemployed, uneducated, irresponsible and using drugs.

It wasn't until I was going through the recovery process and improving the quality of my life that I realized how valuable all my experiences have been.

We are all at different places on our recovery journey and our lives have incredible meaning.

Regardless of what society or the system may tell us, we are all valuable and important people deserving of living good quality lives.

Notes:

Our Lives Have Value Worksheet

1. List two ways that having a mental health struggle impacts your life.

2. List two constructive things that you have learned as a result of living with a mental health struggle.

3. Name three parts of your life that has great meaning for you?

Passing Moments

For a few minutes earlier this week, I felt my life was over. I could feel both my body and my mind tensing up. I envisioned carnage and chaos and it seemed so real. I proceeded to question my life and my place in this world. My frustration was increasing and growing. I was in incredible pain.

I was feeling unreasonable and I could sense that I was about to make some very bad decisions.

Yet, this is my life and I did not need to have things go down that route. Even during my worst and most desperate moments, I must try to make the best possible decision given the circumstances.

So I stepped back, and I took more than a dozen deep breaths and I told myself that I had way too much to live for. I could not in good conscience allow my lifelong struggle for wellness and recovery to end in vain. I chose recovery because recovery chose me.

Recovery lives in every single one of us. Recovery is life, love, future, hope, desire, belief, chance, change, opportunity and so much more.

Recovery is worth living for.

Notes:

Passing Moments Worksheet

1. Why do you choose recovery?

2. Give an example of a time when you felt like giving up and what you did to get through it.

3. List three things that you would like to improve about your life.

Recovery is Wonderful

For eight weeks I have been suffering. I was miserable and tortured. I was locked in a personal hell.

The sky was caving in on me. The sun was no longer bright. The air I was breathing was polluted and stale. My mind was poisoned.

I became consumed with negativity. I felt that there was no hope for me. I thought that my life was finished. I felt that hope no longer existed. I thought my life was over. I dragged myself from place to place attempting to fulfill my responsibilities.

I had lost my ability to laugh and I needed to laugh. I needed to smile and feel joy, so I reached out for support.

On Monday I felt a tiny bit of hope enter my heart.

On Tuesday I worked my butt off to feel better.

On Wednesday I both laughed and smiled even while I still hurt.

Today I hurt a little bit less and I am grateful to be using this Better Days workbook.

My recovery brought me to this workbook. So today I will laugh and smile, for today I am alive and free.

Recovery is wonderful!

Notes:

Recovery is Wonderful Worksheet

1. What two things can you do to keep functioning when you are not well?

2. If you feel that you have lost all hope, which people in your life can you reach out to, and how might those people be helpful?

3. What are three goals that you are working hard at achieving in the next twelve months?

Recovery Planning

Struggling is part of recovery; therefore we all experience tough times. If we learn better ways to manage those tough days in which we are triggered and/or having difficulties, we will be happier and healthier in the long run.

If we learn better ways to nurture our recovery process, we can do better and feel better. We can have more control over how we feel when things are tough.

If we want things to be better, we must make healthy choices to work toward our Better Day.

I know all of this to be true based on my own personal experiences. The reality is that if we want to feel better then we need to work at it.

When we are struggling we can work toward making things better. We can choose to help ourselves move through our recovery process.

We will succeed!

Notes:

Recovery Planning Worksheet

1. Name and explain one method that you currently use to help yourself get back on track when you are having tough times.

2. Give an example of one way that you would like to learn how to help yourself feel better.

3. What does Recovery mean to you?

Staying Strong

When we have a tough day, it can be hard to follow through with all of our responsibilities. On these tough days, we must ask ourselves that if we are not feeling 100%, are we still able to successfully go to our appointments, work, school, social commitments, etc.? Sometimes we need to accept that we have it within ourselves to battle though our difficulties and continue to move forward toward our goals.

In my experience it is absolutely possible to work through difficulty and find wellness and success.

Yesterday was a tough day for me, yet I stayed strong and worked hard and it ended up being an incredibly wonderful day.

Notes:

Staying Strong Worksheet

1. What are three situations that you might choose where it would be better to stay at home when you are not feeling 100%?

2. What are three situations that you might choose to battle through and move forward with your day, even if you are not feeling 100%?

3. Name two situations in which you stuck with your plan and responsibilities for the day and then realized you were feeling better. Why do you think you were feeling better?

Ups and Downs

Every single day I am faced with many challenges. As I live my daily life, there are so many things that I experience that can impact how I am feeling.

Perhaps somebody said something to me that I didn't like or a person on the bus was rude to me.

These kinds of interactions can really impact how I am feeling. I must acknowledge that these ups and downs are part of life and that it is possible to learn how to better handle them. I must always remember that I am the one who chooses how I will react to the difficult situations that I face.

In order to do a better job managing our ups and downs, we can take the first step of believing that it is indeed possible to have a Better Day, hour by hour, minute by minute and second by second.

Notes:

Ups and Downs Worksheet

1. What are three examples of situations where something has really caused you to feel badly?

2. What is the first thing that you would like to improve upon when it comes to managing your daily life and your interactions with others?

3. Do you believe that a Better Day is possible? What are two things that you can do today to make your Better Day a reality?

We Can't Control Everything

The recovery journey can introduce many wonderful experiences into our lives. With that said, there are things that may happen in our daily life that are completely out of our control.

In my experience, I have found that part of living in this world is having to face the fact that I am unable to control all the parts of my life.

Yesterday, I had to face being insulted and having some very hurtful things said to me and about me for something that was not my responsibility in any way. I had no control over the cause of the situation. However, as I was the bearer of some bad news, I became the target.

I hurt. And I hurt a lot.

Then my day went on and my life went on, and it was up to me to accept that there are things that I cannot control, that I have done my very best and that, unfortunately, things don't always work out the way I would like them to. However, my life does go on and I will continue to work as hard as humanly possible to achieve my Better Days.

Notes:

We Can't Control Everything Worksheet

1. Take five minutes and ask a safe person to talk with you about any topic that you are interested in that is unrelated to your struggle. How did this go for you?

2. Then take five minutes and ask that same person how they are doing today. Then ask that person to ask you how you are doing. This is Peer Support.

3. When things happen that are out of your control, what are three things that you can do to help yourself feel better and to have a Better Day?

Being in the Moment

In the past week, my recovery experience has taught me so much. My inner pain is erupting like a volcano and damaging all in my path. This cycle plagues me time and time again and derails my recovery.

No more will I allow myself to give in to the pain and extreme negativity that I feel at times. Never again will I allow myself to suffer without also trying to fight my way out of my pain. I can and I will learn better ways to manage my life when I am struggling.

WE WILL allow our recovery to heal us, and we will grow and live a better quality life. When we struggle, we decide in that moment if we want to make things better. If we want Better Days, we must work hard to have them.

Notes:

Being in the Moment Worksheet

1. What does "Being in the Moment" mean to you?

2. What are three things that you can do when you are struggling so you can start to feel better?

3. Do you believe that it is possible to learn better ways to manage your life? If so, what are three things that you would like to improve about your life?

Dealing with the Impossible

In my life, I have experienced some really unmanageable and difficult situations. I've often felt that, no matter what I do or how hard I try, nothing will ever change for the better. This is extreme and personal pain that, as a person living with a mental health struggle, I am forced to face. It feels like every single day I am forced to deal with impossible to resolve situations, and this triggers me.

This is a battle that drains me of my strength and crushes my motivation.

My reality is that I choose to face the impossibilities in my life and to fight for my Better Days and that's that.

Notes:

Dealing with the Impossible Worksheet

1. List one to three current situations in your life that feels impossible to manage.

2. In what ways can you try to manage what feels like an impossible situation in your life?

3. List three of your personal strengths in dealing with very difficult situations.

Having Patience

Having patience is often very difficult when you are going through the recovery process. The frustrations and unfairness of life can really grind a person down. We work as hard as we can, when we can, to improve the quality of our lives. But sometimes, it feels like getting well and having a good life is impossible, and a lot of people in recovery have felt this at some point in their lives. The recovery process requires having patience. Over time, with hard work on our recovery, we will get there.

We must be patient. Recovery takes time, yet it is worth every bit of time and effort that we put into it.

Notes:

Having Patience Worksheet

1. When you are working through your recovery process, what are some things that can happen that frustrate you?

2. What are two healthy things that you can do as part of your recovery process when you're feeling frustrated and impatient with your life?

3. What is the number one thing that you want to improve in your life and that, with patience, will help you get there?

The Importance of Companionship

As a person who lives with a mental health struggle, I am well aware of how lonely and alone my life can feel at times. I have learned that it is possible to make progress toward improving my relationships. However, this requires hard work.

Why is companionship so important for a person going through the recovery process?

Do you feel that you can count on your peers to be supportive and to listen if you need them to? Let's think about our lives—Are there people in yours that you can reach out to? Perhaps offer support to each other? Perhaps build friendships with?

As people living with a mental health struggle, our lives can feel very alone. We can change this for the better and find happiness, companionship and peace.

Notes:

The Importance of Companionship Worksheet

1. Name one worthwhile friendship that you have in your life. What are the best parts about having this friendship?

2. What does having a good friend mean to you? What does it mean to be a good friend?

3. Why is peer support and friendship so important to have when a person is in the recovery process?

Living the Life You Want to Live

Before 2006, I had never heard of the concept of recovery. I had no idea that people living with mental health issues could get better and live decent lives. I always had so many dreams, goals and aspirations that, unfortunately, had not become reality. This was and is something that is very frustrating for me, and I would imagine that I am not the only person who can relate to this. In order to lead the life I want to live, I need to consider that my dreams and goals are real possibilities so that I can work toward living a happier life day, by Better Day, by Better Day, by Better Day.

With hard work and dedication, you can lead a happier, healthier and more satisfying life.

Notes:

Living the Life You Want to Live Worksheet

1. What are three goals that you have in your life?

2. Do you believe that you could achieve any of your goals?

3. What are two steps that you could take to help yourself achieve your goals?

Meaningful Activities

In order to be happy and healthy, there are a few needs that I must have met in my life. One of those needs is that I must be doing something that has meaning and purpose.

I come to the Boston Resource Center (a peer-led recovery community) once a week because I have the need to be involved in something helpful and productive. As a human being, I feel that I must contribute something of value to society. One of the best parts of my entire week is sitting with my peers engaging in conversation about improving the quality of our lives.

Having purpose is something that I always lacked in my life. I needed to do something more. It was hard to make it happen. However, I have made great progress and I've only just begun.

Notes:

Meaningful Activities Worksheet

1. What are two things that you do in your life that have meaning for you?

2. What are two meaningful activities that you would like to add to your life in the next two years?

3. What steps must you take to add more meaningful activities in your life?

Resiliency

What is Resilience? The Merriam Webster dictionary defines resilience as "an ability to recover from or adjust easily to misfortune or change."

By definition, I am resilient. I am able to recover from extreme hardship and pain. However, being resilient isn't something to be taken for granted. In my opinion, in order to be resilient, a person must have suffered incredible pain, hardship and difficulty. Sadly, life forces us to be resilient, and this happens when we face hardship, pain and difficulty.

The "system" often takes our resiliency for granted, as if we can be treated badly yet expected to bounce back because we always have in the past. We are not robots built to be treated as emotionless beings. We are human beings who deserve to feel joy, pleasure and satisfaction. While we are forced to be resilient, our resiliency can act as a launching pad toward achieving our hopes, dreams and desires.

Notes:

Resiliency Worksheet

1. Do you feel that you are a resilient person? Give one example describing how you are resilient.

2. List two experiences that you have had in your life where you bounced back from an extreme hardship or difficulty.

3. List three hopes, dreams and desires that you want to work toward achieving in your life.

The Little Things

Wow, today I feel both angry and frustrated. I feel like I work so hard to have a better life and to find success, yet I still feel unfulfilled. Sometimes I feel like I just want to give in and stop trying.

It is during these times that I must think about all the little things in my life that make a difference.

These little things are valuable, important and necessary to keep my recovery on track.

What are some examples of the little things in your life that are meaningful and important for you?

Notes:

The Little Things Worksheet

1. What are your top three goals for the next twelve months?

2. What are the little things in your life that help you maintain your recovery?

3. Name three little things that you really enjoy about your daily life.

Time Management

One of the biggest difficulties that I have in my life is managing my time. I struggle with going to bed on time, and I have struggled at times with being on time to my appointments and obligations.

Sometimes, even when I have a lot of time on my hands to get things done, I don't, even if it is something I absolutely need to take care of. Sometimes I don't get to feel the sun shining down on me because I stayed home all day.

How will I make better use of my time so it will benefit my life and my recovery? In what ways can I improve how I manage my time?

Our lives improve by taking baby steps toward living better lives.

Notes:

Time Management Worksheet

1. How will your life improve when you manage your time better?

2. What are two examples of situations where your life was impacted by not making better use of your time?

3. What are three parts of your life that you can improve by managing your time better?

Working through Pain

I've been suffering in pain for nearly two weeks. I keep getting better and then getting worse again.

I've had to force myself to go to school, and be active and social, and follow through with my general daily responsibilities and activities. I know I am not the only person who knows what this suffering feels like. I know that there are others like me who can understand, and who have empathy for me.

How do we get ourselves to eat, sleep, bathe, talk, laugh, love, find peace, find happiness and find our recovery process when it feels lost? How do we find our Better Day? How do we keep moving forward in life when we feel broken or stuck?

Notes:

Working through Pain Worksheet

1. I ask my loved ones and my supporters to remind me that my pain "will pass" when I am suffering. In what ways can people support you to help you when you are suffering?

2. When you're feeling overwhelmed, what are two healthy things you can do to help yourself feel better?

3. What is one thing that you have done this week that you struggled with yet succeeded at accomplishing?

The Value in Our Struggle

I sit here very tired, sick with a cold and feeling useless. It is as if my body continues my struggle toward mental wellness independently of my conscious mind. I think this is because somewhere along my journey to recovery I found hope and promise and options in my struggle. This struggle has never been easy for me. It has been a constant life lesson knocking me down and then helping me up over and over again.

Our struggles have value. The struggles of every person using this workbook are valuable. Our struggles teach us how to live and how to be. Someday we will look back and say thank goodness for the experiences we have had and for how much we have grown, and then we realize that we are strong and we can be proud and we can celebrate our lives.

Notes:

The Value in Our Struggle Worksheet

1. When you feel terrible, unable to function or manage your life, what are two things that you can do to get yourself back on track?

2. What are two things that you can ask someone else to help you with during your times of need?

3. Looking back over your life, what are two experiences in which you have struggled and then found that you had learned a good and helpful lesson?

The Phoenix Will Always Rise

Today was one of the most dreadful days that I have had in quite some time. I can tell you that I am doing ok. However, my history of trauma has caught up with me.

I spent years living in poverty and facing a struggle for my basic security and safety on a daily basis. I have experienced terrible abuse at the hands of the police and other authority figures, such as group home and hospital staff and other mental health providers. I have suffered for no good reason and nevertheless, damage has been done to me.

A few weeks ago I witnessed something violent and I identified and related with the person in crisis. I intervened to support this person and to help calm things down. I saw myself in this person who was experiencing this crisis, and inside my mind and body it felt that I was experiencing the crisis as well.

I have been feeling very strange the past few weeks and I have struggled with knowing the reasons why. I now know what I am feeling. I know that I am dealing with the effects of experiencing trauma so many times in so many ways over so many years of my life.

Today is also a new beginning for me and I will not allow myself to be victimized again. I understand and believe that all of my experiences in my life have important value and have helped me become who I am today. I am grateful for all of my experiences: good, bad and otherwise, and I will always survive and I will continue to fight for my Better Days, baby step by baby step by baby step.

Recovery is a powerful force that is within us all. May we all have Better Days and better lives starting at this very moment.

Notes:

The Phoenix Will Always Rise Worksheet

1. When you are feeling mentally unwell, what are three things that you can do to take care of yourself?

2. List one or two examples of how your life has improved due to dealing with a hardship or a difficult or stressful experience.

3. Complete this statement: To me recovery is…

Doing Something Nice for Yourself

For those of us who live with mental health struggles, our lives can often feel overwhelmed by adversity. When we are going through our recovery process, we can be so focused on taking care of all the aspects of our lives that we want or need to improve, that we often skip enjoying simple pleasures, such as sitting in the sun, reading a good book, going to the movies, going on a picnic or playing with a puppy. For all the hard work we do to nurture our recovery process, we also deserve to laugh and smile because it is so good for our mind, body and soul.

As individuals with mental health struggles, our lives are often very complicated. We are worthy of doing nice things for ourselves, especially while dealing with lives complicated by triggers and frustrations. If we can take some time to do something nice for ourselves, the result is that Better

Days are on the way, and Better Days are here to stay.

Notes:

Doing Something Nice for Yourself Worksheet

1. What are three simple pleasures that make you happy?

2. Why is it important to be gentle to yourself?

3. How will our lives improve by spending time enjoying some simple pleasures?

Expectations

As people living with mental health struggles, we hear the word "expectations" a lot. Everyone has expectations for us, including social workers, family, "staff," doctors, friends, society, etc. We often forget about the expectations that we have for ourselves. We are so busy trying to meet the expectations of others that our own personal needs and desires can get pushed to the side. In this world, we often live without fulfilling our desires, and we owe it to ourselves to work toward achieving some of our own goals and personal expectations. We deserve to have personal standards and to meet those standards.

Notes:

Expectations Worksheet

1. List three expectations that others have placed on you.

2. List three goals that you have for yourself.

3. In order to achieve your goals, what are two steps that you will need to take?

Gratitude List

I have often felt terrible and hopeless. I have often felt that everything was horrible and worthless and that my life was not worth living. I have often felt miserable and useless. I have often felt that nothing will ever change for me.

Fortunately, a good friend of mine introduced me to a really wonderful and helpful way of dealing with my thoughts and feelings. She suggested writing gratitude lists. This basically means that, at those moments when I felt my worst, I can get a pen and paper, think and brainstorm for a few minutes, and write down all the things that I am thankful for. I often end up writing a long list of all the good things. This has been incredibly helpful for me, and I use this coping method all the time. It really helps me.

On some days, in order for me to find my Better Day, I need to really work at it. I write a gratitude list whenever I start to feel bad and even if I have to write a gratitude list every day, I do it. This is something that has helped me survive some of my darkest hours.

Notes:

Gratitude List Worksheet

1. When you are feeling terrible and losing hope, what can you do to help yourself?

2. What are the coping skills that you currently use to find your Better Day?

3. What are all the things that you are grateful for in your life?

Frustration

In my quest to find my Better Day, I am often sidelined by the frustration I experience. In the

Merriam Webster dictionary, frustration is defined as, "a deep chronic sense or state of insecurity and dissatisfaction arising from unresolved problems or unfulfilled needs." This sounds familiar, doesn't it?

For me personally, I find my frustration can be crippling at times. Sometimes, my frustration has made me feel pessimistic and this can be devastating for me. However, I must strive harder and apply my coping skills because as long as the sun still rises every morning, I have an opportunity to fight for my Better Day.

Notes:

Frustration Worksheet

1. What are three productive ways to deal with frustration?

2. Name one situation in your life where something important worked out well for you.

3. How can we take control of our lives and stay on track to reach our goals even when faced with frustration?

Choosing Better Ways to React

When we are having a rough day, how can we get through our day successfully and make it better?

All people have a bad day once in a while, and we can choose to make our "bad day" a Better Day.

We can choose how to react to things that happen in our lives, and we can learn to improve our ability to handle things that happen that we don't like. If we can take more responsibility in making better choices for ourselves, then we can have more control over the quality of our lives.

Notes:

Choosing Better Ways to React Worksheet

Imagine that someone that lives in your household was very loud last night and you were unable to get enough sleep.

1. How would something like this make you feel; how would you react to the noise and the disruption of your sleep?

2. Would your reaction to the noise make things better for you or would your reaction make things worse?

3. Give one example from your life in which you successfully handled a difficult situation.

Getting Upset

Daily life can sometimes be very stressful. Things can often happen that can be upsetting or make us angry. When we get upset or angry, what can we do to successfully move through these emotions and still have a productive day? There are two things we can keep in mind. The first is, we are all able to make better choices. The second is, the better choices we make, the better we feel. We have the ability to change how our day is going to be, even if something happens that sets us off course.

It is helpful to remember that sometimes our feelings are often more intense in the moment. It is very possible that ten, twenty or even thirty minutes later, we may feel differently about the situation we are facing, and we will have moved on with our day. It is important to remember that when we have difficult moments during the day, that we have the potential to still have a good day.

It is also important to think about the concept that we learn from all of our experiences and, with practice in better managing our emotions, we can, step by step, discover the better life we want.

Notes:

Getting Upset Worksheet

1. In what ways can you help yourself step back in the moment and remember that your emotions will soon become more manageable?

2. How can you keep it together in the moments when you feel the worst, so that you can salvage your day?

3. What does is it mean to choose to have a Better Day?

COMMUNITY & PEER SERVICES (CAPS)

RADICAL RECOVERY PEER SUPPORT (RRPS)

Radical Recovery Peer Support is a program that utilizes Peer Support to help individuals achieve wellness and personal growth. The author of the program uses first-person inspirational passages to draw parallels between concepts and recovery. The Program can be done either in-person or online and is conducted as a group.

For the groups, we have three options. The first is a general wellness and personal growth group which is simply called Radical Recovery Peer Support. There is also a group with a focus on higher education called "RRPS-University", and finally there is a version of RRPS for Criminal-reentry called "RRPS-Liberation".

Over the course of five sessions, each group covers important concepts like the Linear Growth Model and Parallel Recovery Concepts. It also focuses on the nine Recovery Fundamentals which include principles like Honesty, Trust, Acceptance, Hope, Personal Responsibility, Self-Advocacy, and others. How each group presents the concepts and fundamentals is unique.

RRPS is a Cognitive Behavioral Therapy. It is such because the description of the Concepts and Fundamentals, as well as the person first descriptions of the recovery journey address beliefs, thoughts, and feelings commonly experienced in a specific but large audience.

The programs also incorporate themes of Rational Emotive Therapy in the different events emphasized in each program. From more general distressing circumstances in the original RRPS, to more specific events such as educational neglect in RRPS-University, and the stigma of having a criminal record in RRPS-Liberation, to our beliefs about these issues, and the consequences for results of those beliefs. **Certificates of completion are available.**

Payment Options

For people who are incarcerated

 We have a correspondence course for people currently in jail or prison. Each of the three programs can be completed for $100. Have payment made out to Dakota Fisher and mail the payment to 1016 Memorial Ave, Williamsport, PA 17701 (include the name of the person participating and the address of the prison). To complete the program, you must be able to send the completed course workbook back to us at the above address. **(Remember to tell us which program you want to join)**

For people who are not incarcerated

 Contact us through email at communityandpeerservices@gmail.com. You can ask us when the next group dates are and we will send you a digital invoice. Cost to participate in group $187.5. The cost for Facilitator training is also $187.50. Books sold separately - $60 including shipping. Order books at www.communitypeerservices.com at the bottom of the homepage!

www.communitypeerservices.com

Experience the Depth.

"Personal experiences and insights on recovery from a person in recovery – Innovative mental health workbooks that ask us insightful questions that help us make sense of complex issues of life."

The Original Peer Support Recovery & Coping Skills Workbook & Curriculum

by Gregorio Lewis

www.communitypeerservices.com |

Experience the Insight.

"Personal experiences and insights on recovery from a person in recovery – Innovative mental health workbooks that ask us insightful questions that help us make sense of complex issues of life."

www.communitypeerservices.com |

www.ingramcontent.com/pod-product-compliance
Lightning Source LLC
Chambersburg PA
CBHW081625100526
44590CB00021B/3608